PEOPLE OF MEXICO

SOUTH OF THE BORDER

Laura Conlon

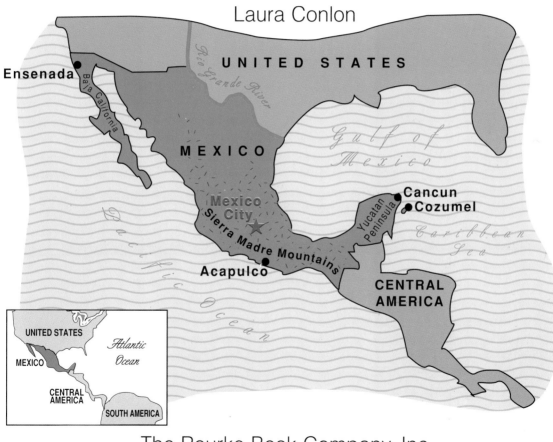

The Rourke Book Company, Inc.
Vero Beach, Florida 32964

Edited by Sandra A. Robinson

PHOTO CREDITS
© James P. Rowan: cover, page 7; © Robert Pelham: page 4;
© Steve Warble: pages 8, 10; © Steve Bentsen: page 12;
© Jerry Hennen: page 21; courtesy Mexico's Ministry of Tourism:
title page, pages 15, 17, 18; © Joseph Antos: page 13

Library of Congress Cataloging-in-Publication Data

Conlon, Laura, 1959-
   People of Mexico / by Laura Conlon.
   p. cm. — (South of the border)
   ISBN 1-55916-052-7
   1. Mexico—Social life and customs—Juvenile literature. I. Title.
II. Series.
F1210.C666   1994
972—dc20   94-11187
                                         CIP

Printed in the USA

TABLE OF CONTENTS

MEXICO: THE PEOPLE

Over 94 million people proudly call themselves Mexicans. Before Spain conquered Mexico in 1521, the native people were mostly from the Mayan and Aztec **cultures.** Today, about one of every three Mexicans is related to these Mayan or Aztec Indians. Most Mexicans are **mestizo,** a mixture of Spanish and Indian. Mexicans are proud of both their past and of modern Mexico.

A group of Indians related to ancient Mayans gather outside a village on Mexico's Yucatan Peninsula

5

HISTORY: THE INDIANS

There were three main **ancient** cultures in Mexico. The first people, the Olmecs, lived over 4,000 years ago. They carved huge stone statues that still stand today.

The Mayans came after the Olmecs, around the year 300 A.D. They built beautiful temples and drew interesting word pictures. The Mayans are a great mystery. No one is sure where they came from or why they vanished around 1100 A.D.

The Aztecs, who followed the Mayans, owned gold and jewels. They created wonderful cities.

El Castillo (*The Castle*) is part of the Mayan ruins at Chichén Itzá on the Yucatan Peninsula

HISTORY: THE SPANISH

Hernando Cortez, a gold-hunter, led the Spanish exploration of Mexico. The Aztec leader Montezuma welcomed Cortez and his men because he thought they were gods. In 1521, the Spanish conquered the Aztecs and destroyed their cities. They called the new land "New Spain."

Three hundred years later, in 1821, Mexicans fought Spain and formed their own country. Mexicans celebrate their Independence Day — which is like Americans' 4th of July — on September 16.

Spanish conquerors brought
Christianity and the Roman Catholic
Church to Mexico and the New World

FAMILY LIFE

The Spanish taught the Mexican people the Spanish language and the Catholic religion. Today Spanish is Mexico's official language, and 97 percent of all Mexicans are Roman Catholic.

Most Mexican families are very close and loving. Often, families have parents, children, grandparents and other relatives all living together. Nothing is more important to Mexicans than their families.

Most Mexican families are close, and households often include many relatives

11

In a land where old and new ways mix, Mexican women launder clothes in a Tamaulipas stream

Modern buildings crowd the waterfront at Puerto Vallarta

FOOD

The most important food in Mexico is corn. *Tortillas* are flat cakes made of corn and baked in a hot pan. Mexicans eat them with almost every meal. Other common Mexican foods are beans, chiles, tacos, peppers and a spicy sauce called *mole*.

Mexicans eat their main meal in the early afternoon. They usually eat a light dinner late in the evening.

Peppers and chiles give a hot, spicy taste to many Mexican meals

CLOTHING

Mexicans who live in large cities dress like people who live in the United States and Canada.

In **rural** areas, more **traditional,** colorful clothing is worn. It is traditional to wear a wool blanket over clothes. Women wear shawls for warmth and for carrying children. Large hats, called **sombreros,** protect people against the sun and rain.

Mexican dancers wear colorful, traditional clothing, including the man's sombrero

RECREATION

The most popular sport in Mexico is soccer. Bullfighting also attracts many people. One of Mexico's proudest events in sports came in 1968, when the Olympic Games were held in Mexico City.

Mexicans love music and dancing. **Mariachis** are strolling, or walking, musicians who play at parties or celebrations.

On weekly market days in rural areas, people walk, shop and visit in town squares.

Guitars, trumpets and violins make lively Mexican music

HOLIDAYS

Mexicans enjoy many **fiestas**, or parties. They celebrate Christmas for nine days. Part of the Christmas celebration is breaking the piñata. The piñata is a papier-mâché animal filled with candy and toys. Children hit the piñata with a stick until it breaks. Then they can gather up the treats.

Each village honors a chosen saint on Saints' Days. These celebrations may last as long as 10 days.

Mexicans celebrate several holidays and fiestas

MEXICO TODAY

Mexico is a mixture of old and new. In some villages, life is much like it was hundreds of years ago. Modern cities have modern problems. The city is crowded and many people are very poor. Mexico City, the capital, has terrible air pollution.

The Mexican people work to solve modern problems while celebrating their proud past.

Glossary

ancient (AIN chent) — very old

culture (KULT cher) — a group of people's way of life

fiesta (fee ESS tah) — the Spanish word for "feast" or "festival"; any kind of party

mariachi (mar ree AH chee) — a strolling musician in Mexico

mestizo (mess TEE soh) — a Mexican who is related to both Spanish and Indian people

piñata (peen YAH tah) — a papier-mâché figure filled with goodies for children

rural (ROOR uhl) — in the country

sombrero (soam BRAY roh) — any kind of hat

traditional (tra DISH uh nul) — referring to things that are done today as they were in the past, usually handed down

23

INDEX